THE
OXFORD
First
ATLAS

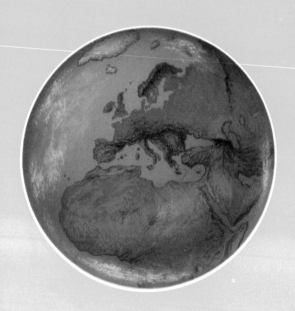

Acknowledgements

The publishers would like to thank the following
for permission to reproduce photographs

Earth Images pp.4, 8, 16; Chris Fairclough pp.10, 28, 41;
FLPA pp.24, 28; Robert Harding p.40;
Hunting Aerofilms Ltd. p.26; Hutchison Library p.29;
Impact: Steve Benbow p.24, Robert Eames p.10,
Jean Hutchings p.10; Magnum Photos pp.42, 44;
Mark Mason Studios p.5; Mountain Camera:
Chris Bradley p.42, John Cleare pp.10, 28,
Colin Monteath p.29;
National Remote Sensing Centre (Airphotogroup) pp.2, 22;
Panos Pictures: Trygve Bolstad p.42;
Sealand Photography Ltd. p.26; Still Pictures pp.10, 44;
ZEFA p.10.

The globes on page 5 were supplied by
Cambridge Publishing Services.

The illustrations are by Chapman Bounford, Hardlines,
and Jon Riley.

Page design by Adrian Smith.

Oxford New York
Athens Auckland Bangkok Bombay
Calcutta Cape Town Dar es Salaam Delhi
Florence Hong Kong Istanbul Karachi
Kuala Lumpur Madras Madrid Melbourne
Mexico City Nairobi Paris Singapore
Taipei Tokyo Toronto

and associated companies in
Berlin Ibadan

Oxford is a trade mark of Oxford University Press

ISBN 0 19 831794 8 (paperback)   ISBN 0 19 831833 2 (hardback)

Printed in Italy by G. Canale & C. S.p.A. - Borgaro T.se - TURIN

Editorial Adviser

Patrick Wiegand

Oxford University Press

2 Contents

Maps of the British Isles

Maps of the United Kingdom

Contents 3

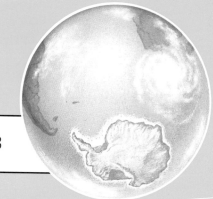
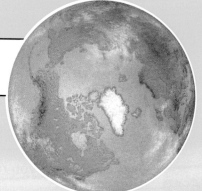

4 Planet Earth

The Earth is a **planet** in space.

It is round like a ball.

If you look at the Earth from space you can see land, sea and clouds.

You cannot see countries.

To see countries you need a map.

There are imaginary lines round the Earth. These help us describe where places are.

Some of the lines have special names.

The line around the middle of the Earth is called the **Equator**.

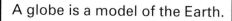

A globe is a model of the Earth.

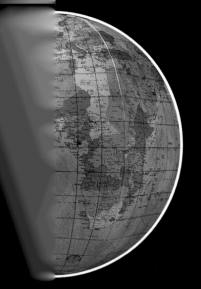

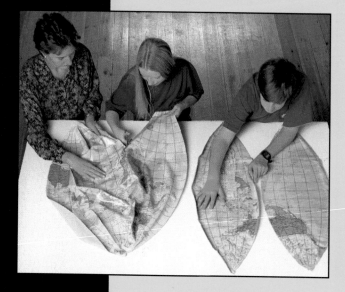

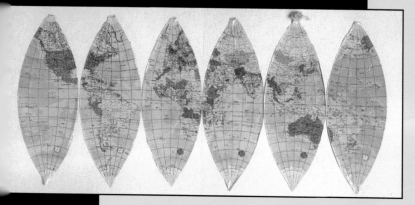

These strips have been cut from a globe and laid flat.

They make a world map.

The map is not easy to use because there are gaps in it.

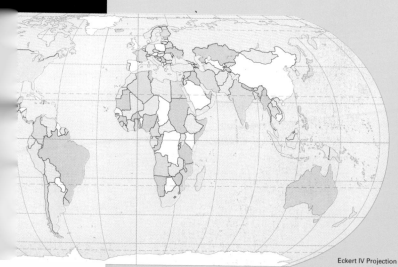

Here is a better world map. Some of the land shapes have had to be stretched.

A world map like this does not show Antarctica very well.

So Antarctica is shown here on a separate map.

Eckert IV Projection

Key

CANADA   names of countries are shown in capital letters

Some countries are too small to be named on the map. They are shown by the first few letters of their name:

A	ALBANIA
AR	ARMENIA
AU	AUSTRIA
AZ	AZERBAIJAN
B	BELGIUM
BD	BRUNEI DARUSSALAM
BE	BENIN
BH	BOSNIA-HERZEGOVINA
BU	BURKINA
C	CROATIA
CAR	CENTRAL AFRICAN REPUBLIC
CZ	CZECH REPUBLIC
G	THE GAMBIA
G-B	GUINEA-BISSAU
H	HUNGARY
IS	ISRAEL
L	LEBANON
LI	LITHUANIA
LU	LUXEMBOURG
M	MACEDONIA, FYR
N	NETHERLANDS
Q	QATAR
R	ROMANIA
S	SLOVAKIA
SL	SLOVENIA
SW	SWITZERLAND
T	TAJIKISTAN
TU	TURKMENISTAN
U	UGANDA
UAE	UNITED ARAB EMIRATES
Y	YUGOSLAVIA
ZIM	ZIMBABWE

These colours are used to show where one country ends and another begins

sea and lakes

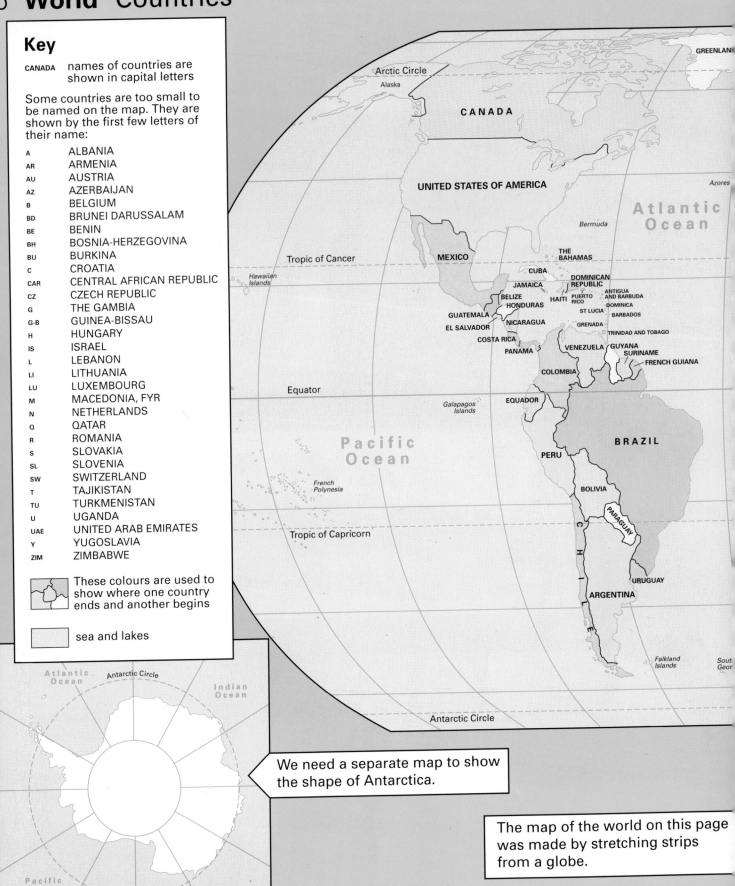

We need a separate map to show the shape of Antarctica.

The map of the world on this page was made by stretching strips from a globe.

Eckert IV Projection
© Oxford University Press

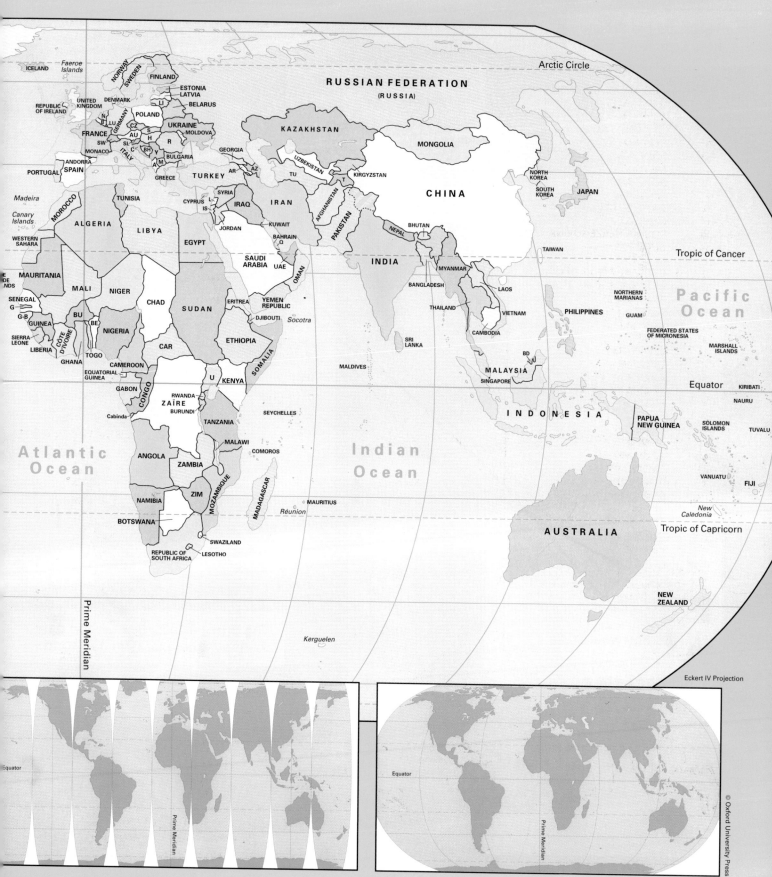

ICELAND
Faeroe Islands
Arctic Circle
NORWAY
SWEDEN
FINLAND
ESTONIA
LATVIA
DENMARK
REPUBLIC OF IRELAND
UNITED KINGDOM
LI
BELARUS
POLAND
N
B
LU
CZ
UKRAINE
GERMANY
S
MOLDOVA
FRANCE
AU
H
R
SW
SL
C
BH
Y
MONACO
ITALY
A
M
BULGARIA
ANDORRA
GREECE
AR
AZ
PORTUGAL
SPAIN
TURKEY
GEORGIA
RUSSIAN FEDERATION
(RUSSIA)
KAZAKHSTAN
MONGOLIA
NORTH KOREA
SOUTH KOREA
JAPAN
Madeira
MOROCCO
TUNISIA
CYPRUS
IS
SYRIA
IRAQ
IRAN
UZBEKISTAN
TU
T
KIRGYZSTAN
AFGHANISTAN
PAKISTAN
CHINA
BHUTAN
NEPAL
Canary Islands
ALGERIA
LIBYA
EGYPT
JORDAN
KUWAIT
BAHRAIN
Q
SAUDI ARABIA
UAE
OMAN
INDIA
TAIWAN
Tropic of Cancer
WESTERN SAHARA
NDS
MAURITANIA
MALI
NIGER
CHAD
SUDAN
ERITREA
YEMEN REPUBLIC
DJIBOUTI
Socotra
MYANMAR
BANGLADESH
LAOS
NORTHERN MARIANAS
Pacific Ocean
SENEGAL
G
G-B
GUINEA
BU
BE
NIGERIA
CAR
ETHIOPIA
THAILAND
VIETNAM
PHILIPPINES
GUAM
SIERRA LEONE
LIBERIA
COTE D'IVOIRE
GHANA
TOGO
CAMEROON
EQUATORIAL GUINEA
GABON
CONGO
ZAÏRE
U
RWANDA
BURUNDI
KENYA
SOMALIA
MALDIVES
SRI LANKA
CAMBODIA
BD
FEDERATED STATES OF MICRONESIA
MARSHALL ISLANDS
Equator
KIRIBATI
Cabinda
TANZANIA
SEYCHELLES
MALAYSIA
SINGAPORE
INDONESIA
PAPUA NEW GUINEA
NAURU
SOLOMON ISLANDS
TUVALU
Atlantic Ocean
ANGOLA
ZAMBIA
MALAWI
COMOROS
Indian Ocean
VANUATU
FIJI
NAMIBIA
ZIM
MOZAMBIQUE
MADAGASCAR
Réunion
MAURITIUS
New Caledonia
Tropic of Capricorn
BOTSWANA
SWAZILAND
LESOTHO
AUSTRALIA
REPUBLIC OF SOUTH AFRICA
Prime Meridian
NEW ZEALAND
Kerguelen
Eckert IV Projection

Equator

Prime Meridian

Equator

Prime Meridian

8 How big are the British Isles?

These are the British Isles seen from space.

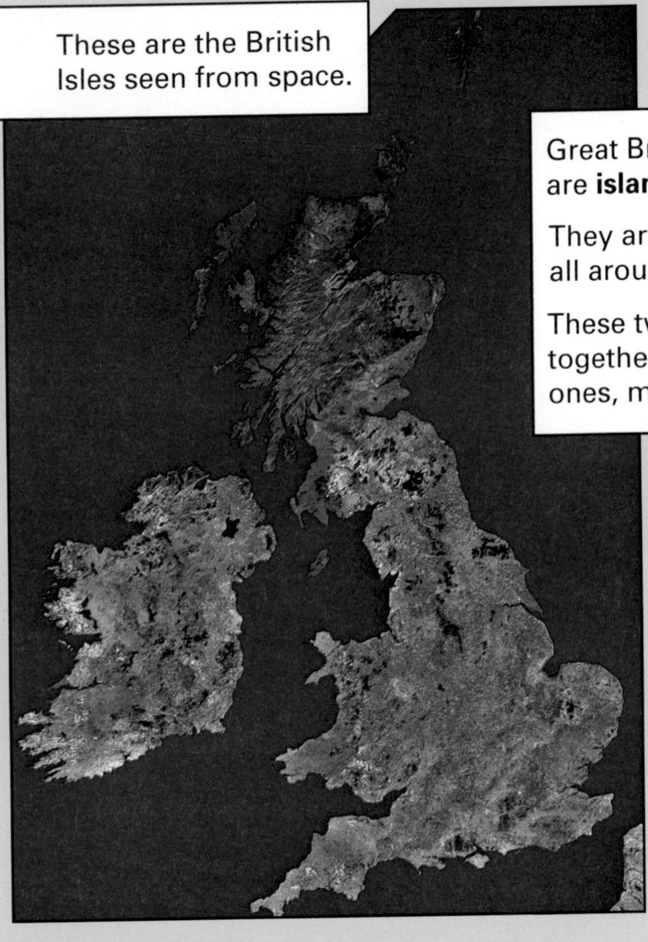

Great Britain and Ireland are **islands**.

They are land with sea all around.

These two large islands, together with many small ones, make the **British Isles**.

Ireland

Great Britain

John o'Groats

It is about 1000 kilometres from John o'Groats to Land's End, as the crow flies.

This journey would take:

about **2 hours** by air

about **2 days** by car

about **40 days** to walk

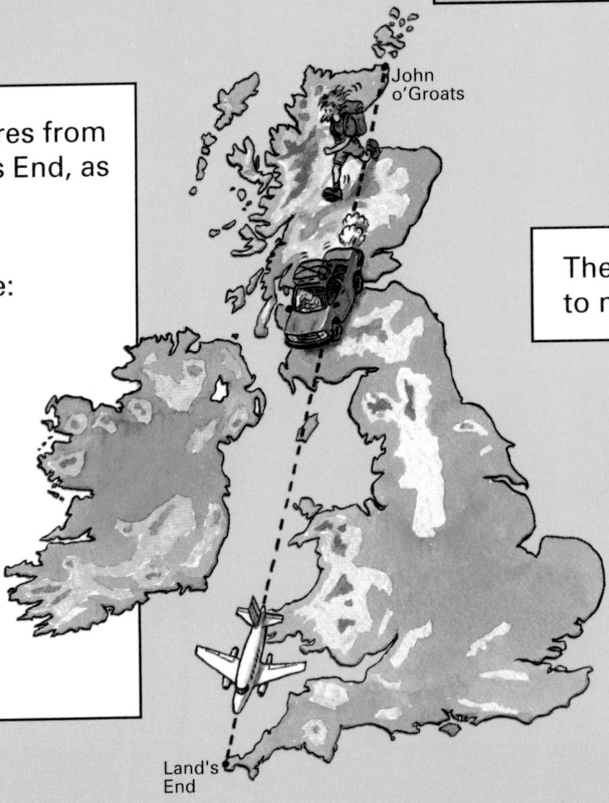

The British Isles are small compared to many other places in the world.

Land's End

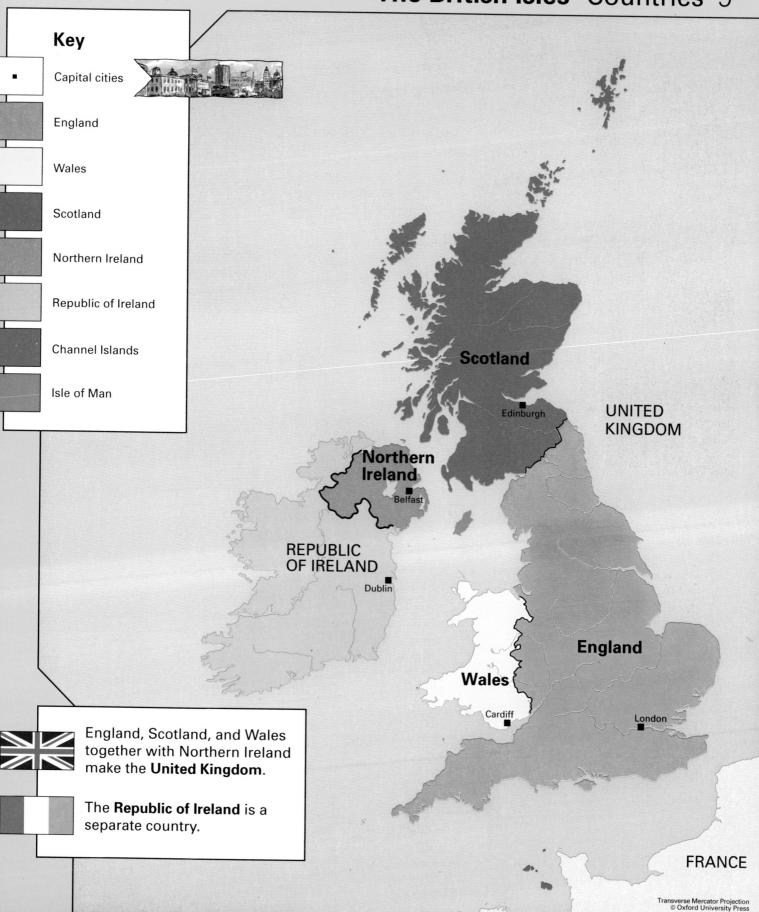

Key

- ■ Capital cities
- England
- Wales
- Scotland
- Northern Ireland
- Republic of Ireland
- Channel Islands
- Isle of Man

England, Scotland, and Wales together with Northern Ireland make the **United Kingdom**.

The **Republic of Ireland** is a separate country.

Scotland

Edinburgh ■

UNITED KINGDOM

Northern Ireland

Belfast ■

REPUBLIC OF IRELAND

Dublin ■

England

Wales

Cardiff ■

London ■

FRANCE

Transverse Mercator Projection
© Oxford University Press

10 Rivers, hills, and mountains

highest peaks

from these you can
see a long way in all
directions

mountains

steep, rocky slopes

moors and uplands

high, wind-swept
places with heather
and rough grass

hills

smooth slopes and
gentle valleys

low lands

mostly flat, marshy
land with wide rivers

rivers

rainwater runs downhill
to collect in rivers which
flow to the sea

Key

▲	highest peaks
	mountains
	moors and uplands
	hills
	low lands
	rivers
	sea

N

NORTHWEST HIGHLANDS

Great Glen

River Spey

GRAMPIAN MOUNTAINS

River Dee

Ben Nevis ▲

River Clyde

SOUTHERN UPLANDS

River Tweed

North Sea

River Tyne

LAKE DISTRICT

Scafell Pike ▲

PENNINES

NORTH YORK MOORS

River Aire

ATLANTIC

OCEAN

River Erne

ANTRIM MOUNTAINS

River Bann

Lough Neagh

Slieve Donard ▲

Irish Sea

Lough Corrib

River Shannon

River Liffey

WICKLOW MOUNTAINS

River Barrow

Snowdon ▲

CAMBRIAN MOUNTAINS

River Severn

River Trent

River Wye

River Avon

River Great Ouse

CHILTERN HILLS

COTSWOLD HILLS

River Thames

BRECON BEACONS

River Blackwater

Carrauntoohill ▲

NORTH DOWNS

EXMOOR

SOUTH DOWNS

DARTMOOR

English Channel

Transverse Mercator Projection
© Oxford University Press

12 Our weather in summer

very warm

warm

cool

very wet   wet   dry

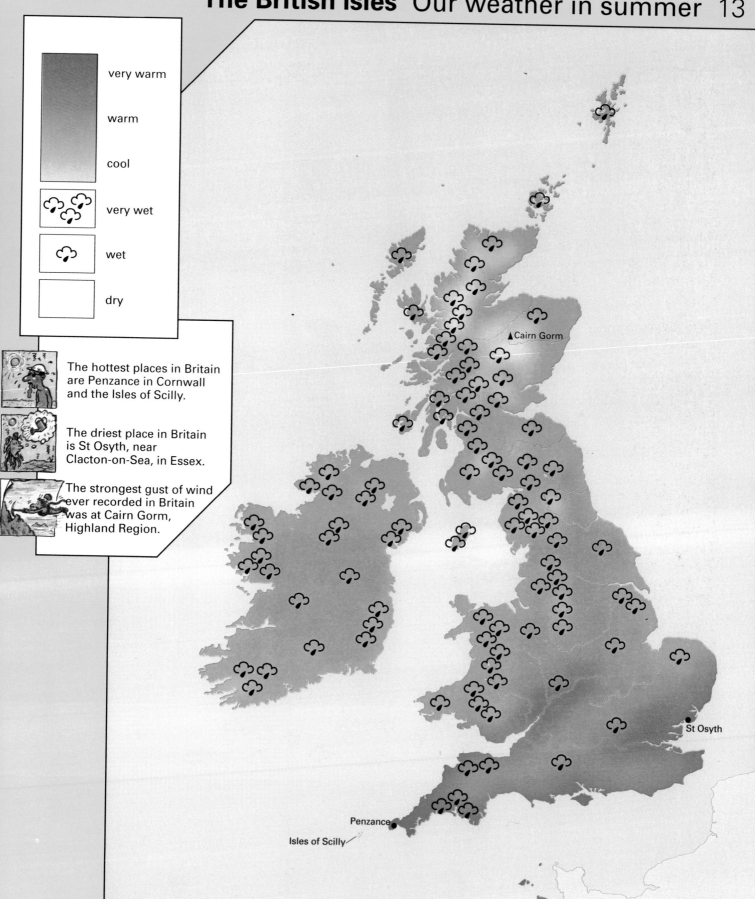

very warm

warm

cool

very wet

wet

dry

The hottest places in Britain are Penzance in Cornwall and the Isles of Scilly.

The driest place in Britain is St Osyth, near Clacton-on-Sea, in Essex.

The strongest gust of wind ever recorded in Britain was at Cairn Gorm, Highland Region.

▲Cairn Gorm

St Osyth

Penzance

Isles of Scilly

Transverse Mercator Projection
© Oxford University Press

The British Isles Our weather in winter

cool
cold
very cold
very wet
wet
dry

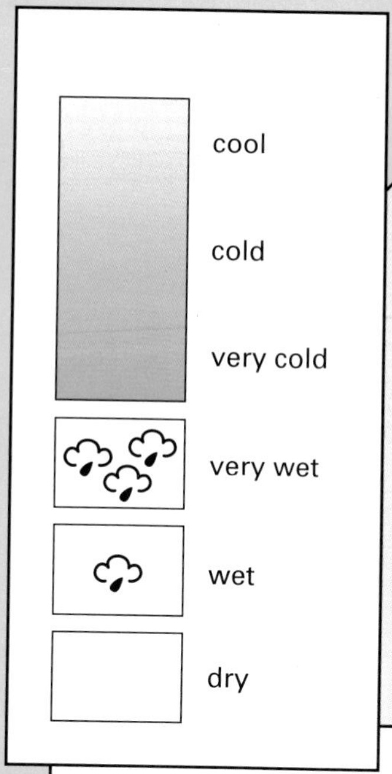

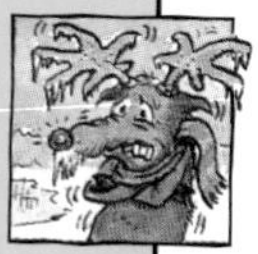

The coldest place in Britain is Braemar, Grampian.

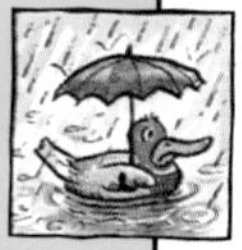

The wettest place in Britain is Sty Head Tarn, near Scafell Pike, in Cumbria.

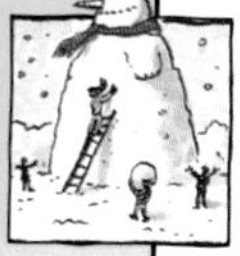

The snowiest places in Britain are Upper Teesdale and the hills of North Wales near Denbigh.

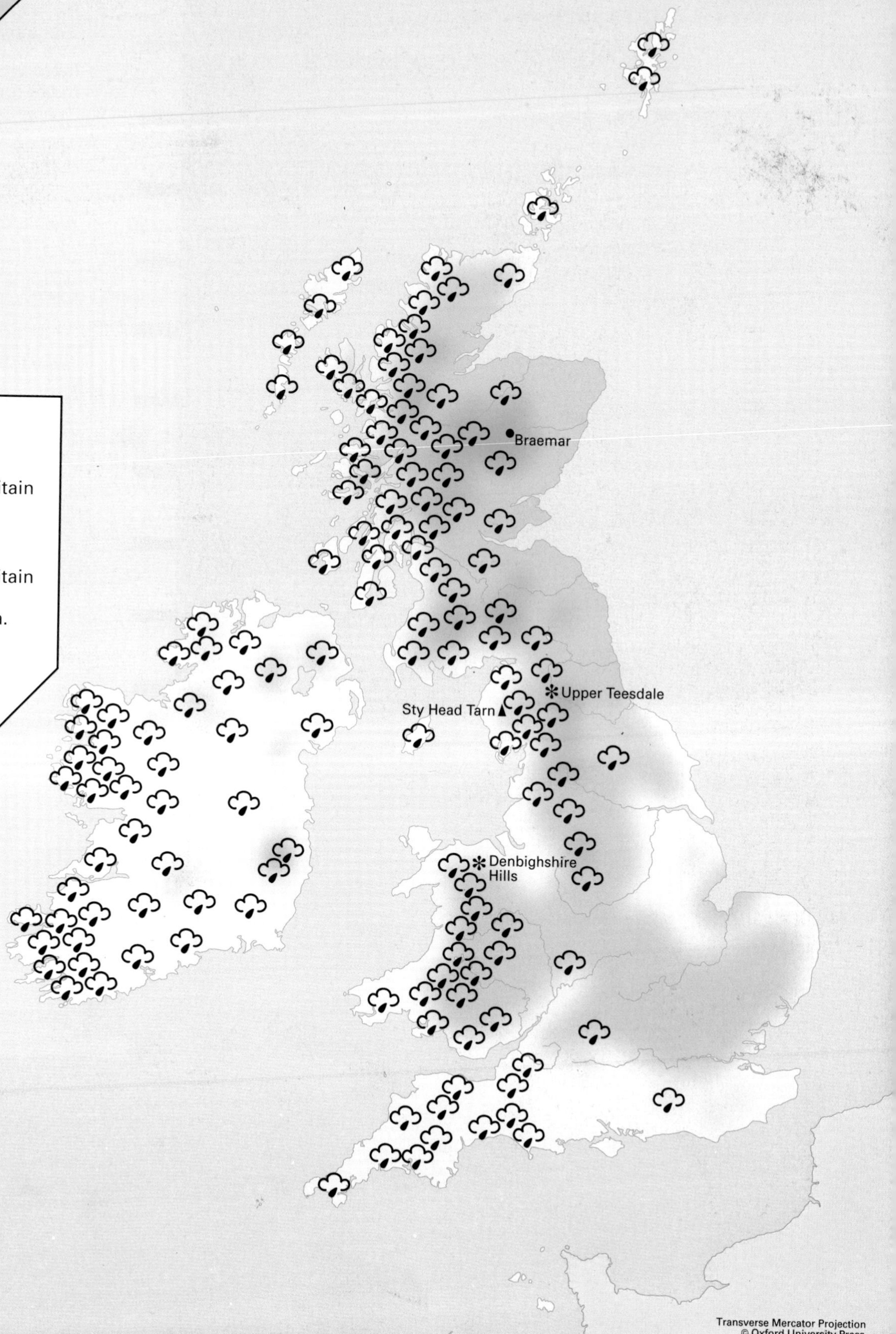

Braemar
Upper Teesdale
Sty Head Tarn
Denbighshire Hills

Transverse Mercator Projection

16 A picture from space

Pictures from space show lots of detail but it is hard to see each town and road.

Maps pick out the most important places and show their names.

Key

lines marking the edge of a country	
motorways and major roads	
railway	
⊕ main airport	
· town	
● large town	
largest built-up area	
river	
lake	
▲ peak or highest point	
mountains	
moors and uplands	
hills	
low lands	
land below sea level	

Transverse Mercator Projection
© Oxford University Press

A T L A N T I C   O C E A N

N

Shetland Islands

Herma Ness
Unst
Fetlar
Yell
Out Skerries
Whalsay
Mainland
Bressay
Foula
Scalloway
Lerwick

Sumburgh Head

Fair Isle

Papa Westray
North Ronaldsay
Westray
Rousay
Sanday
Eday
Stronsay
Orkney Islands
Mainland
Shapinsay
Stromness
Kirkwall
Hoy
South Ronaldsay
Pentland Firth

Rona

Cape Wrath

Duncansby Head
John o' Groats
Thurso
Wick
River Thurso

N o r t h   S e a

Butt of Lewis

Ben More Assynt 998m

Loch Shin

Dornoch Firth

Stornoway
Lewis

The Minch

Clisham 799m

Outer Hebrides

Harris
Scalpay

NORTHWEST HIGHLANDS

Ullapool
Sgurr Mor 1109m
Ben Wyvis 1046m

Tarbat Ness

Moray Firth

Pabbay
Berneray
Little Minch

North Uist

Dingwall

Elgin

Fraserburgh

Benbecula

Portree
Raasay

Inverness

Peterhead

South Uist

Skye
CULLIN HILLS 1009m

Kyle of Lochalsh
Carn Eige 1183m

Loch Ness

River Spey
River Deveron

River Don

Barra

Canna

Fort Augustus

Aviemore

CAIRNGORMS

✈ **Aberdeen**

Rhum
Eigg

Mallaig

MONADHLIATH MOUNTAINS

Ben Macdui 1310m

River Dee

Mingulay

Inner Hebrides

Fort William
Ben Nevis 1344m

Braemar

River North Esk

GRAMPIAN MOUNTAINS

River South Esk

Great Glen

Coll
Tiree

Montrose

Ulva

Ben Cruachan 1126m

Loch Rannoch
Loch Tay
River Tay

Forfar

Mull

Loch Linnhe

SIDLAW HILLS

Arbroath

Iona

Oban

S C O T L A N D

Perth
Dundee

Colonsay
Jura

Loch Awe
Loch Fyne

Loch Lomond

River Forth

St Andrews

Firth of Lorn

Stirling

Glenrothes

Kirkcaldy

Firth of Forth

© Oxford University Press

A **B** **C** **D** **E** **F** **G** **H**

ATLANTIC
OCEAN

N

5

4

3

2

1

Iona Mull
Firth of Lorn
Colonsay Jura Sound of Jura Loch Awe Loch Fyne Loch Lomond River Forth Stirlin
R. Ea
Islay Greenock Cumbernau
Dumbarton Clydeban Paisley Motherw
Bute Hamilton
Glasgow East
Goat Fell 874m Arran Irvine Kilbride
Campbeltown Ayr Kilmarnock
Mull of Kintyre Girvan Cumnoc
SOUTHERN SCO
Stranraer Castle Douglas Dalbeatt
Wigtown Kirkcudbright
Mull of Galloway
North Channel
Isle of Man Snaefell 621m
Douglas

Malin Head
Rathlin Island
Errigal Mountain 752m
Aran Island Letterkenny Coleraine Ballymoney
Lough Foyle Londonderry Ballymena Larne
Lifford SPERRIN MOUNTAINS 683m Sawel ANTRIM MOUNTAINS Carrickfergus
Ballybofey Strabane NORTHERN Antrim Newtownabbey
Donegal Omagh Cookstown Lough Neagh Belfast Bangor
Donegal Bay R. Erne Dungannon Newtownards
Ballyshannon Portadown R. Lagan Lisburn Strangford Lough
Erris Head Lower Lough Erne Enniskillen Armagh Lurgan Downpatrick
Sligo Upper Lough Erne Monaghan IRELAND Banbridge Slieve Donard
Ballina Collooney Lough Allen Newry MOURNE MOUNTAINS 852m
Lough Conn Belturbet Castleblayney Warrenpoint
Newport R. Moy Boyle Cavan Cootehill Dundalk
Carrick-on-Shannon Carrickmacross Louth Dundalk Bay
Castlebar Longford Kells Irish Sea
Westport Claremorris Castlerea Lough Ree R. Boyne Drogheda
Lough Mask Ballinrobe Roscommon Ballymahon Navan Balbriggan
Tuam R. Suck Mullingar
Lough Corrib Athlone Swords
Galway Ballinasloe Tullamore R. Liffey Dublin Amlwch
Galway Bay R. Shannon Banagher Mountmellick Dún Laoghaire Holyhead Llandud
Aran Islands Birr Portlaoise Naas Bray Conwy
Lough Derg Roscrea Kildare Anglesey Bang
Ennis REPUBLIC OF IRELAND R. Barrow WICKLOW MOUNTAINS Caernar
Kilkee Killaloe Nenagh 926m Wicklow Snowdon 1085m
Kilrush SILVERMINE MOUNTAINS Carlow Lugnaquilla Pwllheli
Loop Head River Shannon Templemore Tullow Arklow
Limerick Thurles R. Slaney Gorey Dolgellau
Listowel Kilkenny Barmouth
Newcastle West Cashel R. Nore Enniscorthy 892m Cader Idris
Tralee Tipperary Cahir R. Suir Carrick-on-Suir Cardigan Bay
Dingle 920m Galtymore Clonmel New Ross Wexford Aberystwyth
Killorglin Kanturk Michelstown Waterford Rosslare
Dingle Bay Fermoy New Quay
Carrauntoohill 1041m Killarney Mallow Dungarvan Carnsore Point
MACGILLYCUDDY'S REEKS River Blackwater Cardigan
River Kenmare River Lee Cork Youghal St George's Channel Fishguard Llandover
Bantry Bay Bandon Cobh St David's Head Carmarthen R. Tywi
Mizen Head Bantry Clonakilty Milford Haven
Skibbereen Old Head of Kinsale

B **C** **D** **E** **F** **G** **H**

J Perth
St Andrews
Glenrothes
Kirkcaldy
Dunfermline
kirk
Edinburgh
Livingston
Clyde
LAMMERMUIR HILLS
UPLANDS
Galashiels
Broad Law ▲840m
Moffat
Hawick
LAND
CHEVIOT HILLS
Kielder Water
mfries
Carlisle
The Cheviot 815m
River Coquet
Morpeth · Blyth
Hexham
Tynemouth
Newcastle upon Tyne
Gateshead · **Sunderland**
Consett Washington
· Durham
Cross Fell 893m
Penrith
River Wear
· Hartlepool
· Redcar
Stockton-on-Tees
Middlesbrough
Whitby
rkington
Keswick
Ullswater
LAKE DISTRICT 978m Scafell Pike
Windermere
Kendal
PENNINES
Darlington
Richmond
Northallerton
NORTH YORK MOORS
· Scarborough
Whernside 737m ▲
River Ure
Ripon
River Nidd
Malton
YORKSHIRE WOLDS
Flamborough Head
Bridlington
arrow-in-urness
Morecambe
Lancaster
Harrogate
Skipton
York
River Wharfe
R. Ouse
R. Derwent
Fleetwood
Blackpool
Lytham St Anne's
Southport
Preston
R. Ribble
Bradford
Halifax
Leeds
Castleford
ENGLAND
Kingston upon Hull
River Humber
Spurn Head
Chorley
Blackburn
Rochdale
Bury
Huddersfield
R. Aire
Scunthorpe
Grimsby
Bolton
Oldham
Louth
iverpool
kenhead
Widnes
Wigan
Warrington
Manchester
Stockport
Doncaster
R. Trent
Mablethorpe
LINCOLN WOLDS
Runcorn
Macclesfield
Buxton
Mersey
Rotherham
Sheffield
Worksop
Lincoln
Skegness
wyn
Chester
Crewe
R. Derwent
Chesterfield
Matlock
Newark-on-Trent
Boston
Denbigh
Wrexham
River Dee
Llangollen
Oswestry
Stafford
Stoke-on-Trent
Ilkeston
Arnold
Derby
Burton upon Trent
Nottingham
Grantham
The Wash
Long Eaton
Loughborough
Spalding
THE NENE FENS
R. Welland
R. Trent
R. Soar
Coalville
Leicester
R. Nene
Wisbech
Shrewsbury
Telford
Cannock
Walsall
Corby
Peterborough
Kettering
Ely
Thetford
River Waveney
R. Severn
Wolverhampton
Bridgnorth
West Bromwich
Dudley
Birmingham
Coventry
Newtown
Kidderminster
Solihull
R. Great Ouse
Bury St Edmunds
R. Teme
Redditch
Rugby
Warwick
Northampton
Bedford
Cambridge
Ipswich
R. Wye
Great Malvern
Worcester
R. Avon
Stratford-upon-Avon
Evesham
Banbury
Milton Keynes
River Stour
Harwich
Hay-on-Wye
Hereford
COTSWOLD HILLS
Cheltenham
Aylesbury
Luton
Welwyn Garden City
Colchester
St Osyth
recon
BLACK MOUNTAINS
CONS
Monmouth
R. Usk
Gloucester
R. Severn
Cirencester
R. Thames
R. Cherwell
CHILTERN HILLS
R. Lea
Harlow
Chelmsford
Merthyr Tydfil
Pontypool
Oxford
London

North Sea

Firth of Forth
St Abb's Head
Berwick-upon-Tweed
River Tweed
Holy Island
River Esk
River Tyne
R. Tyne
R. Tees
R. Swale
R. Lune
R. Ribble
River Witham

Key

∿	lines marking the edge of a country
≈	motorways and major roads
▬	railway
⊕	main airport
·	town
●	large town
⬤	largest built-up area
∿	river
◌	lake
▲	peak or highest point
■	mountains
■	moors and uplands
■	hills
■	low lands
■	land below sea level

REPUBLIC OF IRELAND

Transverse Mercator Projection
© Oxford University Press

© Oxford University Pres

A B C D E F G H

6

Irish Sea

Lough Ree
Athlone
Mullingar
Navan
Swords
R. Boyne
Tullamore
Dublin
R. Liffey
Dún Laoghaire
Amlwch
Holyhead
Llandudno
Conwy
Colwyn Bay Widnes
Chorley
Southport
Bolton Bury Rochdale Oldham Huddersfield
Wigan
Liverpool
Birkenhead
Warrington
Manchester
Stockport
Doncast
Sheffi

REPUBLIC
OF
IRELAND
Birr
Roscrea
Naas
Kildare
Portlaoise
R. Barrow
R. Nore
Bray
WICKLOW
MOUNTAINS
Anglesey
Bangor
Caernarfon
Snowdon
1085m
Denbigh
Wrexham
River Dee
Llangollen
Runcorn
Macclesfield
Chester
Crewe
Buxton
Stoke-
on-Trent
R. Derwent
Matloc
Ilkeston
Arn

5
Nenagh
Lough Derg
SILVERMINE
MOUNTAINS
R. Shannon
Thurles
Cashel
Tipperary
Kilkenny
Carlow
Tullow
R. Slaney
▲926m
Lugnaquilla
Wicklow
Arklow
Gorey
Pwllheli
Dolgellau
Barmouth
892m
Cader
Idris
Oswestry
Stafford
Shrewsbury
Telford
Wolverhampton
Bridgnorth
R. Severn
R. Vyrnwy
Derby
Burton
upon
Trent
R. Trent
Cannock
Coal
Walsall
West Brom
Birmingha
920m
Galtymore
Cahir
R. Suir
Clonmel
Carrick-
on-Suir
Waterford
New
Ross
Enniscorthy
Wexford
Rosslare
Cardigan
Bay
Aberystwyth
New Quay
W A L E S
CAMBRIAN MOUNTAINS
Newtown
Kidderminster
R. Teme
Dudley
Solihull
Redditch
Worcester
R. Avon
Rugb
Warwic
Coven

Dungarvan
Youghal
Carnsore
Point
St George's Channel
St David's Head
Cardigan
Fishguard
Carmarthen
R. Teifi
R. Tywi
Llandovery
Brecon
BRECON
BEACONS
BLACK
MOUNTAINS
Hay-on-
Wye
Hereford
R. Wye
Great Malvern
R. Usk
Evesham
Cheltenham
Stratford-
upon-Avon
Banbury
HILLS
R. Cherwell
Oxf

4
ATLANTIC
Milford
Haven
Llanelli
Swansea
Port Talbot
Neath
Merthyr
Tydfil
Rhondda
Caerphilly
Pontypool
Cwmbran
Monmouth
Stroud
Gloucester
COTSWOLD
R. Thames
Cirencester
R. Severn
Oxf
Bridgend
Barry
Cardiff
Newport
Bristol
Weston-
super-
Mare
Bath
Trowbridge
R. Avon
Swindon
Newbury
Basingsto

OCEAN
Bristol
Channel
Lundy
Ilfracombe
Hartland Point
Minehead
EXMOOR
R. Exe
Barnstaple
R. Taw
QUANTOCK
HILLS
Bridgwater
MENDIP
HILLS
R.
R. Parrett
R. Yeo
Yeovil
R. Stour
SALISBURY
PLAIN
Salisbury
R. Avon
R. Test
Winchester
Eastle
Taunton
Tiverton
Lyme
Regis
Dorchester
Southampton
Farehа
Portsmout

3
Trevose Head
Newquay
BODMIN
MOOR
River Tamar
Yes
Tor
619m
DARTMOOR
River Teign
R. Dart
Exeter
Exmouth
Lyme Bay
Weymouth
R. Frome
Poole
Portland
Bill
Bournemouth
Swanage
Isle of Wi

N
St Ives
Truro
St Austell
Plymouth
Dartmouth
Torbay
Start Point
Penzance
Land's End
Falmouth
Isles of
Scilly
Lizard Point

2
English Channel
Alderney
Cap de la Hague
Channel
Islands
St Peter-
Port
Sark
Guernsey
Cherbou
Valog
Jersey
St Helier
Carentan
Coutances
H

B C D E F G H

Key

	lines marking the edge of a country
	motorways and major roads
	railway
⊕	main airport
·	town
●	large town
	largest built-up area
	river
	lake
▲	peak or highest point
	mountains
	moors and uplands
	hills
	low lands
	land below sea level

REPUBLIC of IRELAND

Map labels:

J K L M N 6

Scunthorpe
Grimsby
Spurn Head
R. Trent
River Humber
LINCOLN WOLDS
Louth
Mablethorpe
Lincoln
Newark-on-Trent
River Witham
Skegness
Wells-next-the-Sea
Boston
Cromer
The Wash
King's Lynn
River Bure
Spalding
THE FENS
Wisbech
River Wensum
R. Welland
R. Nene
Great Yarmouth
Norwich
Lowestoft
Corby
Peterborough
Thetford
River Waveney
Southwold
Kettering
R. Great Ouse
Ely
Bury St Edmunds
Northampton
Cambridge
Aldeburgh
Bedford
ENGLAND
River Stour
Ipswich
Milton Keynes
Felixstowe
Harwich
Luton
Colchester
Harlow
St Osyth
Welwyn Garden City
CHILTERN HILLS
St Albans
Chelmsford
Watford
Slough
Basildon
London
Southend-on-sea
Reading
Gravesend
Sheerness
Margate
Gillingham
Canterbury
Woking
Reigate
Redhill
Maidstone
Deal
NORTH DOWNS
Bedford
Crawley
R. Medway
Ashford
Dover
Horsham
THE WEALD
Royal Tunbridge Wells
Folkestone
R. Arun
SOUTH DOWNS
Havant
Brighton
Hastings
Strait of Dover
Bognor Regis
Worthing
Eastbourne
Newhaven
Beachy Head

North Sea

Ostend
Nieuwpoort
BELGIUM
Dunkerque
Calais
Poperinge
Cassel
St-Omer
Boulogne-sur-Mer
Armentières
Lillers
le Touquet-Paris-Plage
Montreuil-sur-Mer
Bruay-en-Artois
Lens
Berck-Plage
Hesdin
Arras
Doullens
le Tréport
Abbeville
River Somme
Dieppe
St Valery-en-Caux
Blangy-sur-Bresle
Amiens
St Quentin
Fécamp
Etretat
Neufchâtel-en-Bray
Poix-de-Picardie
Roye
Montdidier
Bolbec
Yvetot
Forges-les-Eaux
Laon
Noyon
le Havre
Honfleur
Gournay-en-Bray
Beauvais
Compiègne
Deauville-les-Bains
Pont-Audemer
Rouen
Clermont
Oise
Soissons
Bayeux
FRANCE
Gisors
River Seine
Caen
Cabourg
Lisieux
Louviers
R. Seine
Senlis
Château-Thierry
Evreux
Vernon
Paris
Meaux

e de la Seine

J K L M N

Transverse Mercator Projection
© Oxford University Press

22 Where people live

Large towns and built-up areas have lots of houses, schools, shops, offices, and factories.

This photograph shows part of Leicester.

Most people in Britain live and work
in large towns and built-up areas.

Key

∿	lines marking the edge of a country
∿	river
•	large town
⬭	largest built-up area
■	capital city

Aberdeen

Scotland

Glasgow **Edinburgh**

Northern Ireland

Belfast

Newcastle upon Tyne

Sunderland

UNITED KINGDOM

REPUBLIC OF IRELAND

Leeds

Bradford Kingston upon Hull

Liverpool Manchester

Sheffield

Stoke-on-Trent

Nottingham

Derby

Wolverhampton Leicester Norwich

Birmingham Coventry

Wales **England**

Cardiff

Bristol

London

Southampton

Plymouth

FRANCE

Transverse Mercator Projection
© Oxford University Press

farmland

farmers use the land to produce food by growing crops and keeping animals

forest

forest land is used to grow trees for timber

coast

much land at the edge of the sea is used for holidays

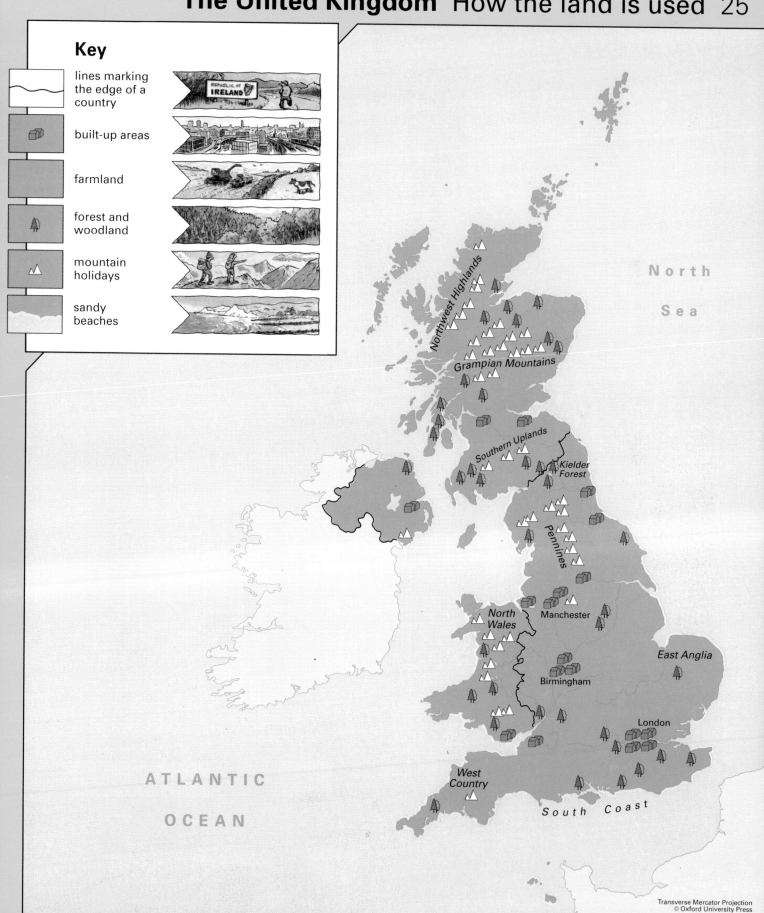

Key

lines marking the edge of a country

built-up areas

farmland

forest and woodland

mountain holidays

sandy beaches

REPUBLIC of IRELAND

North Sea

Northwest Highlands

Grampian Mountains

Southern Uplands

Kielder Forest

Pennines

North Wales

Manchester

East Anglia

Birmingham

London

West Country

South Coast

ATLANTIC

OCEAN

Transverse Mercator Projection
© Oxford University Press

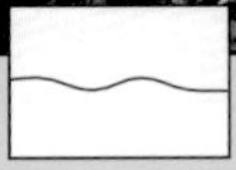

railway

motorway

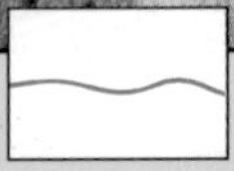

airport

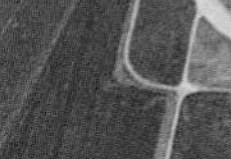

port

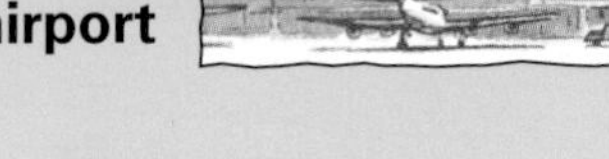

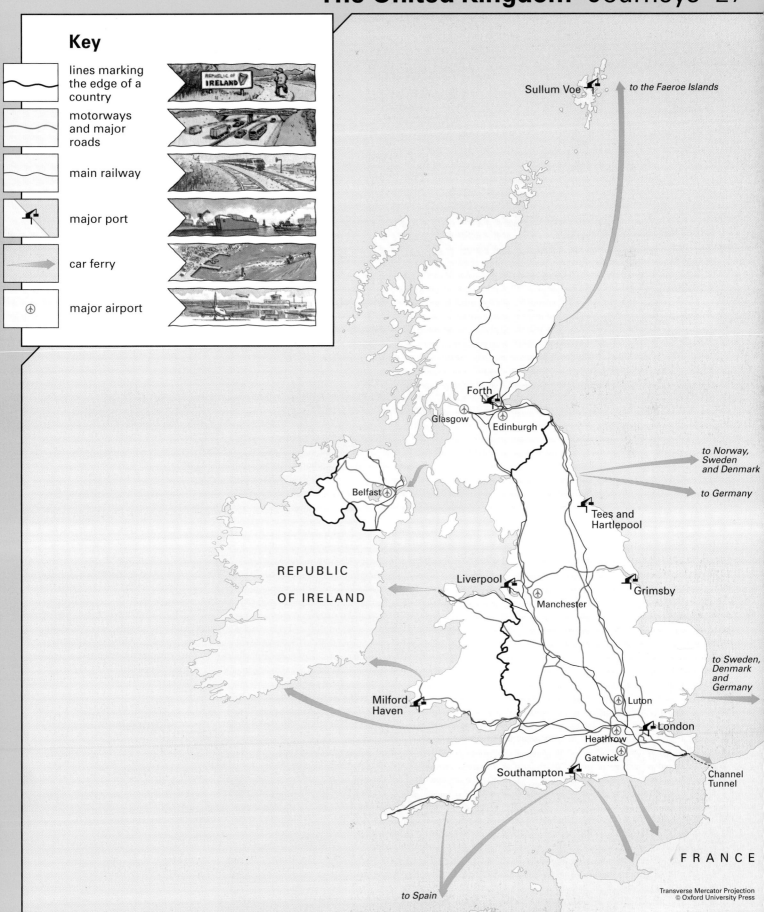

Key

lines marking the edge of a country	
motorways and major roads	
main railway	
major port	
car ferry	
major airport	

Sullum Voe

to the Faeroe Islands

Forth

Glasgow

Edinburgh

to Norway, Sweden and Denmark

to Germany

Belfast

Tees and Hartlepool

REPUBLIC OF IRELAND

Liverpool

Manchester

Grimsby

to Sweden, Denmark and Germany

Milford Haven

Luton

London

Heathrow

Gatwick

Channel Tunnel

Southampton

FRANCE

to Spain

Transverse Mercator Projection
© Oxford University Press

mountains

desert

savannah

marsh

hot forest

cold forest

The photographs show different environments.
They are our natural surroundings.

The matching symbols are used on the maps on pages 30-39.

 ice and icebergs

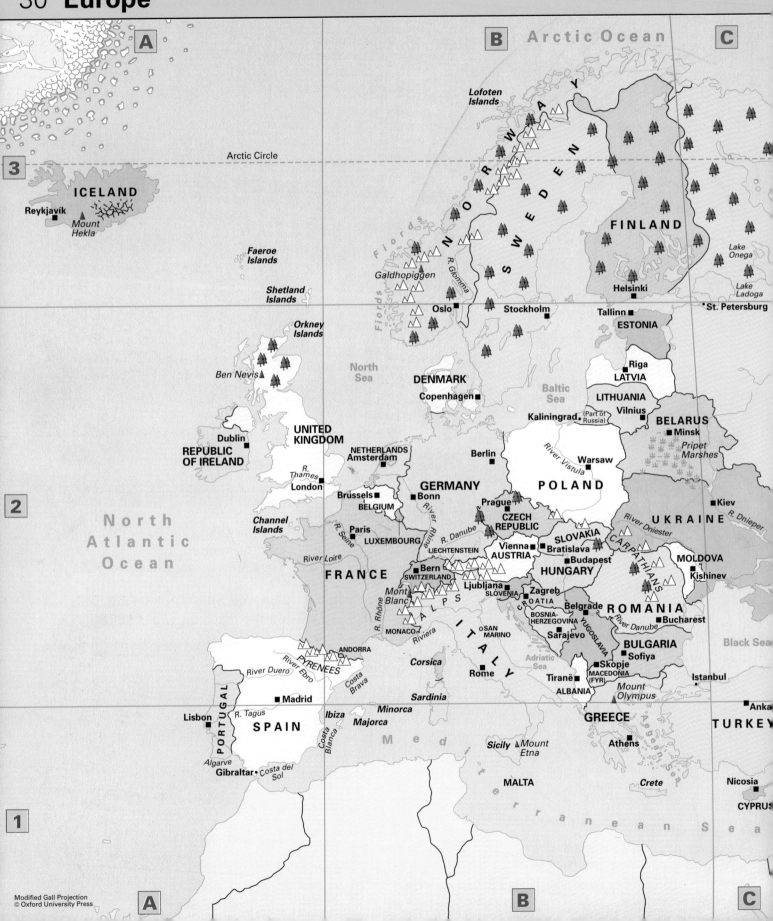

Arctic Ocean

A

B

C

Lofoten Islands

Arctic Circle

3

ICELAND

Reykjavík

Mount Hekla

Faeroe Islands

Shetland Islands

Galdhøpiggen

R. Glomma

N O R W A Y

S W E D E N

FINLAND

Lake Onega

Helsinki

Oslo

Stockholm

Tallinn

Lake Ladoga

St. Petersburg

ESTONIA

Orkney Islands

Ben Nevis

North Sea

DENMARK

Copenhagen

Baltic Sea

Riga

LATVIA

LITHUANIA

Kaliningrad *(Part of Russia)*

Vilnius

BELARUS

Minsk

Pripet Marshes

North Atlantic Ocean

Dublin

REPUBLIC OF IRELAND

UNITED KINGDOM

R. Thames

London

NETHERLANDS

Amsterdam

Brussels

BELGIUM

Berlin

GERMANY

Bonn

River Vistula

Warsaw

POLAND

Kiev

UKRAINE

River Dnieper

Prague

CZECH REPUBLIC

River Rhine

2

Channel Islands

R. Seine

Paris

LUXEMBOURG

LIECHTENSTEIN

River Rhine

R. Danube

Vienna

AUSTRIA

Bratislava

SLOVAKIA

Budapest

HUNGARY

CARPATHIANS

River Dniester

MOLDOVA

Kishinev

River Loire

FRANCE

R. Rhône

Bern

SWITZERLAND

Mont Blanc

A L P S

Ljubljana

SLOVENIA

Zagreb

CROATIA

Belgrade

ROMANIA

Bucharest

River Danube

MONACO

Riviera

I T A L Y

SAN MARINO

BOSNIA-HERZEGOVINA

Sarajevo

YUGOSLAVIA

BULGARIA

Sofiya

Black Sea

ANDORRA

Pyrenees

River Ebro

Corsica

Rome

Adriatic Sea

Skopje

MACEDONIA (FYR)

Tiranë

ALBANIA

Mount Olympus

Istanbul

Anka

River Duero

PORTUGAL

R. Tagus

Lisbon

Madrid

SPAIN

Ibiza

Minorca

Majorca

Costa Blanca

Costa Brava

Sardinia

GREECE

Athens

TURKEY

Algarve

Gibraltar

Costa del Sol

Sicily

Mount Etna

MALTA

Crete

Nicosia

CYPRUS

M e d i t e r r a n e a n   S e a

1

A

B

C

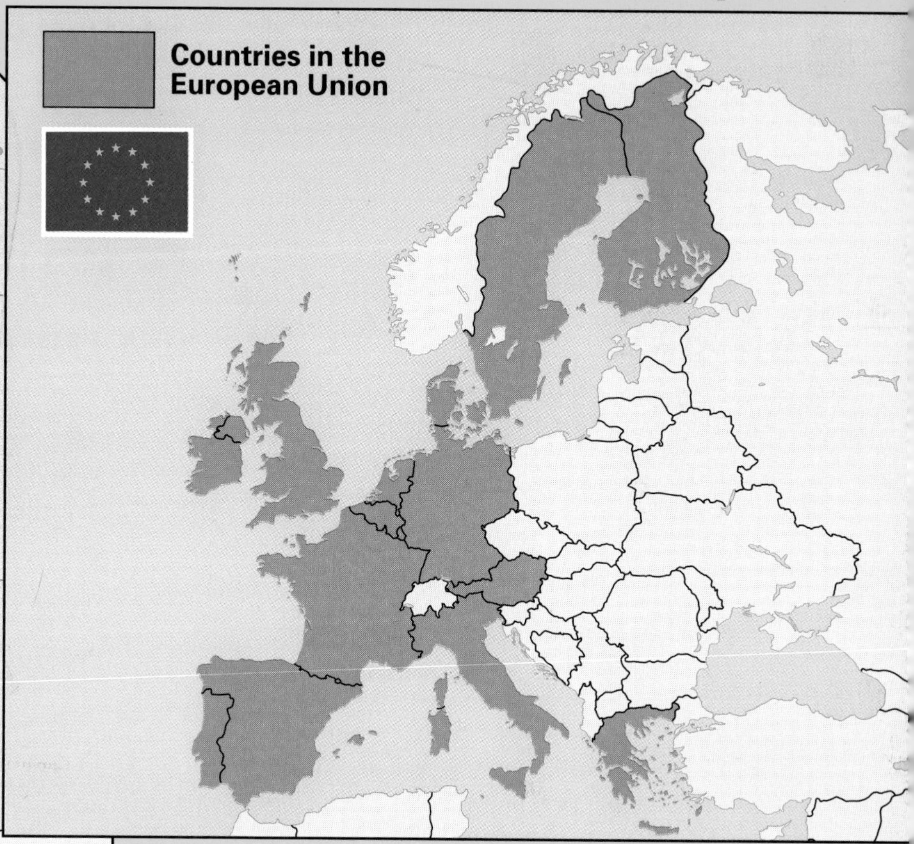

C

Arctic Ocean

Barents
Sea

D

3

North Dvina River

U R A L   M O U N T A I N S

RUSSIAN FEDERATION
(RUSSIA)

River Volga

Moscow

**Countries in the
European Union**

2

Aral
Sea

Mount
Elbrus
CAUCASUS

GEORGIA

■Tbilisi

Caspian
Sea

TAURUS
MOUNTAINS

Key

ITALY	names of countries are in capital letters		marsh
■	capital cities		ice on land / ice on sea
•	other big cities		icebergs
	the biggest rivers		
▲	the highest peaks		
⌃⌃	mountains		
🌲	cold forest		

C

1

D

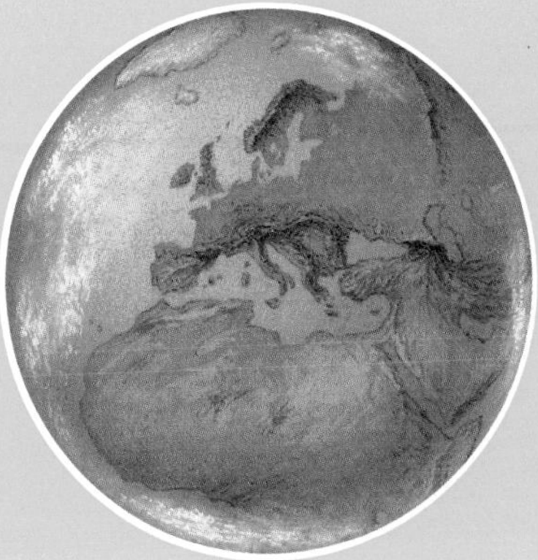

Modified Gall Projection
© Oxford University Press

Barents Sea

Arctic Circle

■ Moscow

River Volga

URAL MOUNTAINS

River Ob

RUSSIAN FEDERATION (RUSSIA)

River Yenisey

River Angara

River Lena

Lake Baykal

Sea of Okhots

KAZAKHSTAN

River Irtysh

Lake Balkhash

ALTAI MOUNTAINS

Aral Sea

MONGOLIA

Ulan Bator ■

GOBI DESERT

Black Sea

CAUCASUS

Caspian Sea

ARMENIA

Yerevan ■
Mount Ararat ▲

Baku ■
AZERBAIJAN

Almaty ■

Tashkent ■

UZBEKISTAN

Bishkek ■
KIRGYZSTAN

River Hwang Ho

Beijing ■

Tientsin •

NORTH KOREA
Pyongyang ■

Sea of Japan

JAPA

TURKMENISTAN

Dushanbe ■

Communism Peak ▲
TAJIKISTAN

Seoul •

SOUTH KOREA

Mount Fuji▲

Tokyo ■

Ashkhabad ■

Mount Demavend ▲

Mount K2 ▲

CHINA

Honshu

R. Tigris

R. Euphrates

Tehran ■

AFGHANISTAN

Kabul ■

JAMMU AND KASHMIR

Yellow Sea

Shikoku
Kyushu

Beirut ■
LEBANON

SYRIA

Damascus ■

Baghdad ■

IRAN

Islamabad ■

TIBETAN PLATEAU

R. Mekong

R. Salween

Yangtze River

Shanghai •

ISRAEL

Amman ■

IRAQ

New Delhi ■

HIMALAYAS

Chungking •

Jerusalem ■
JORDAN

KUWAIT

PAKISTAN

R. Indus

Mount Everest ▲

NEPAL

Ryukyu Islands

Kuwait City ■

BAHRAIN

Kathmandu ■

BHUTAN
Thimpu ■

Taipei ■

Riyadh ■

QATAR

R. Ganges

Dhaka ■

R. Irrawaddy

HONG KONG

TAIWAN

Tropic of Cancer

SAUDI ARABIA

UNITED ARAB EMIRATES

Muscat ■

BANGLA DESH

Calcutta ●

Red Sea

OMAN

Bombay ●

INDIA

MYANMAR

Hanoi ■

The Gulf

Arabian Sea

Bay of Bengal

WESTERN GHATS

Vientiane ■

LAOS

VIETNAM

South China Sea

Manila ■

San'a ■

YEMEN REPUBLIC

Rangoon ●

THAILAND

Bangkok ■

PHILIPPINES

Mount Nabi Shu'ayb ▲

Socotra

Andaman Islands

CAMBODIA

Phnom Penh ■

Mount Kinabalu ▲

SEYCHELLES

Colombo ■

SRI LANKA

Nicobar Islands

MALAYSIA

BRUNEI DARUSSALAM

Bandar Seri Begawan ■

MALDIVES

Kuala Lumpur ■

SINGAPORE

Borneo

Celebes

Jaya Peak ▲

Equator

Sumatra

Java Sea

INDONESIA

Jakarta ■

Java

Indian Ocean

Christmas Island

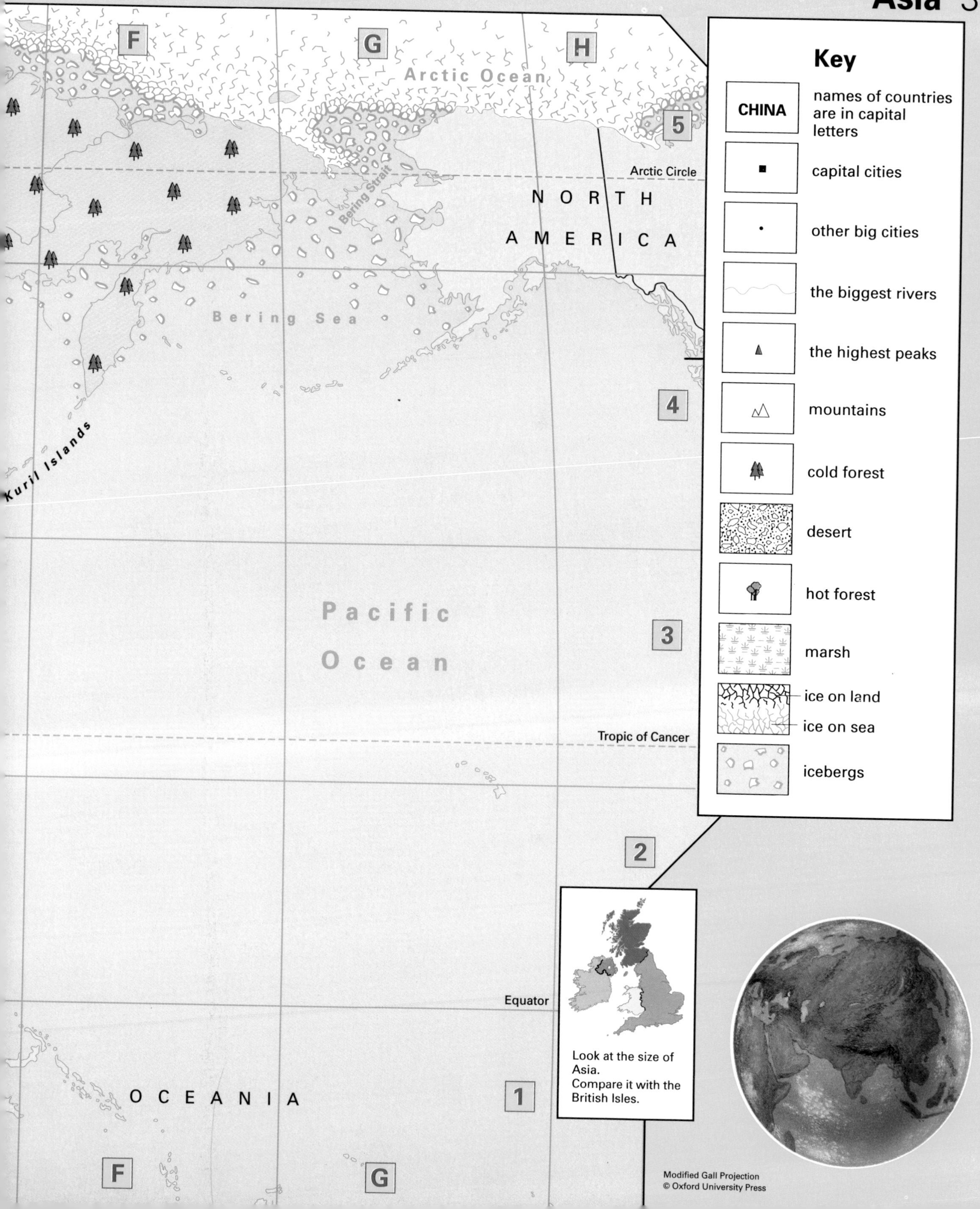

F G H

Arctic Ocean

5

Arctic Circle

N O R T H

A M E R I C A

Bering Strait

Bering Sea

4

Kuril Islands

Pacific

3

Ocean

Tropic of Cancer

2

Equator

1

O C E A N I A

F G

Key

CHINA	names of countries are in capital letters
■	capital cities
·	other big cities
～	the biggest rivers
▲	the highest peaks
⌃	mountains
🌲	cold forest
	desert
🌳	hot forest
	marsh
	ice on land
	ice on sea
	icebergs

Look at the size of Asia.
Compare it with the British Isles.

Modified Gall Projection
© Oxford University Press

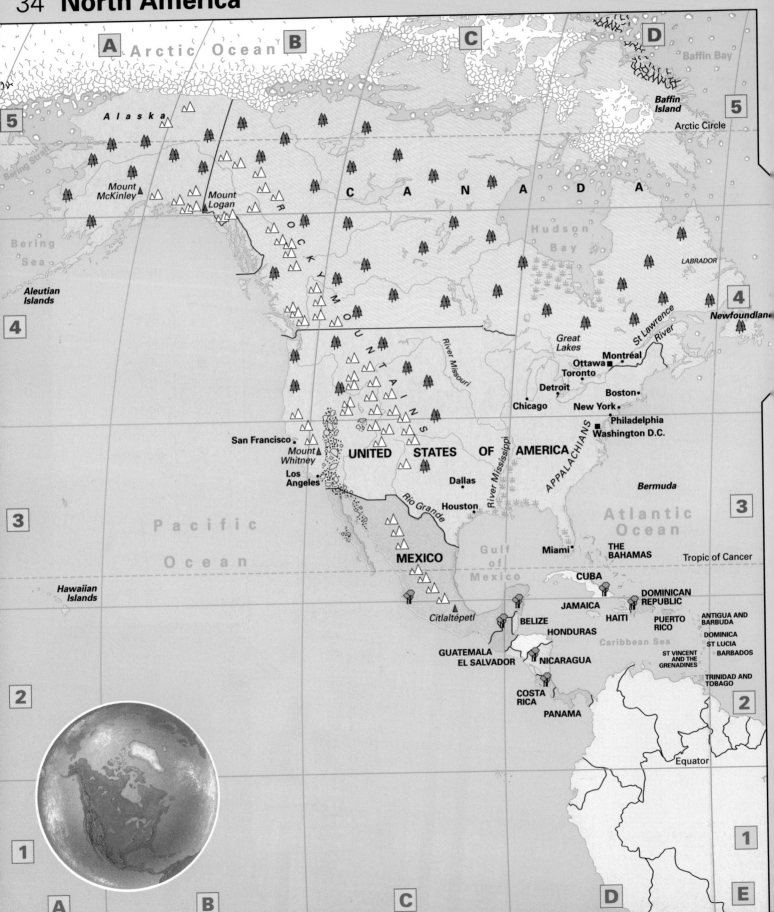

A **B** **C** **D**

Arctic Ocean

Baffin Bay

5

Baffin Island

Arctic Circle

Alaska

Bering Strait

Mount McKinley

Mount Logan

C A N A D A

Hudson Bay

LABRADOR

5

Bering Sea

R
O
C
K
Y

Aleutian Islands

4

M
O
U
N
T
A
I
N
S

Great Lakes

St Lawrence River

Newfoundland

4

Montréal

Ottawa

Toronto

Detroit

River Missouri

UNITED   STATES   OF   AMERICA

Chicago

Boston

New York

Philadelphia

Washington D.C.

APPALACHIANS

San Francisco

Mount Whitney

Los Angeles

Dallas

Houston

Rio Grande

River Mississippi

Bermuda

Atlantic Ocean

3

3

Pacific

Ocean

MEXICO

Gulf of Mexico

Miami

THE BAHAMAS

Tropic of Cancer

Hawaiian Islands

CUBA

Citlaltépetl

BELIZE

JAMAICA

HONDURAS

HAITI

DOMINICAN REPUBLIC

PUERTO RICO

ANTIGUA AND BARBUDA

DOMINICA

ST LUCIA

BARBADOS

Caribbean Sea

ST VINCENT AND THE GRENADINES

2

GUATEMALA

EL SALVADOR

NICARAGUA

TRINIDAD AND TOBAGO

2

COSTA RICA

PANAMA

Equator

1

1

A **B** **C** **D** **E**

Key

CUBA — names of countries are in capital letters

■ capital cities

· other big cities

～ the biggest rivers

▲ the highest peaks

⛰ mountains

🌲 cold forest

desert

savannah

hot forest

marsh

ice on land
ice on sea

icebergs

Look at the size of North America and the size of South America. Compare them with the British Isles.

Modified Gall Projection
© Oxford University Press

Tropic of Cancer

Atlantic Ocean

Caracas
VENEZUELA
River Orinoco
Georgetown
Paramaribo
GUYANA
Cayenne
SURINAME
Bogotá
FRENCH GUIANA
COLOMBIA
ANDES
Quito
ECUADOR
Cotopaxi
Chimborazo
Galapagos Islands

Equator

River Amazon

BRAZIL

PERU
ANDES
Lima

Lake Titicaca
La Paz
BOLIVIA
Brasília
River Paraguay
PARAGUAY
River Paraná
Rio de Janeiro
Tropic of Capricorn
São Paulo
Asunción

Pacific Ocean

ATACAMA DESERT
ANDES
Mount Aconcagua
URUGUAY
Juan Fernandez Islands
Santiago
Buenos Aires
Montevideo
CHILE
ARGENTINA

Atlantic Ocean

Stanley
Falkland Islands

Southern Ocean
Cape Horn

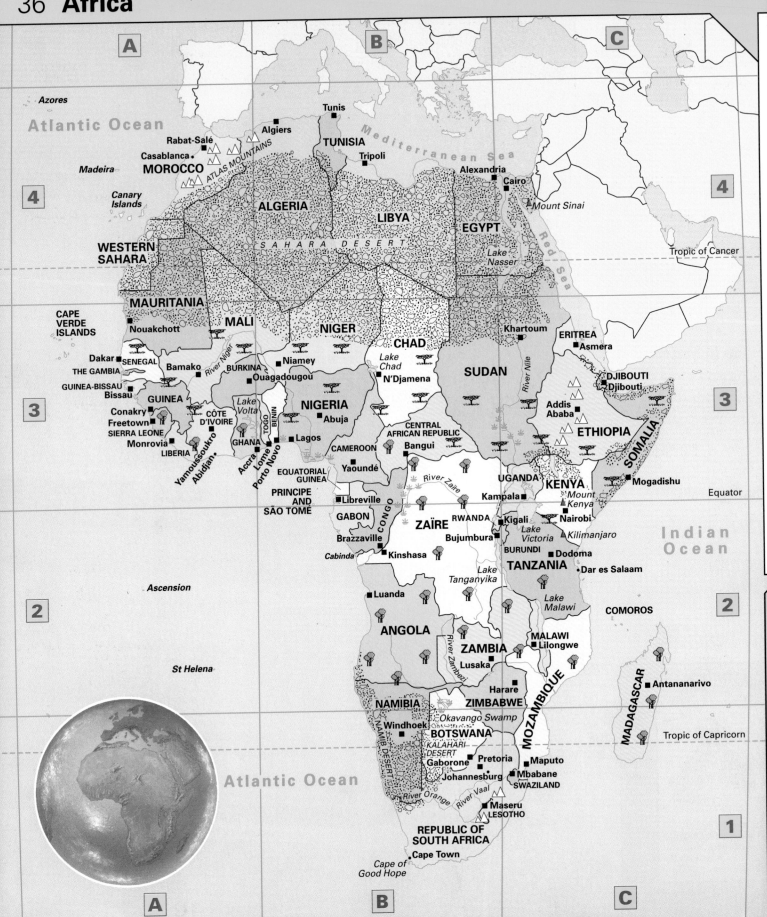

Azores

Atlantic Ocean

Tunis
Algiers
Rabat-Salé
Casablanca
Madeira
MOROCCO
ATLAS MOUNTAINS
TUNISIA
Mediterranean Sea
Tripoli

Canary
Islands

ALGERIA
LIBYA
Alexandria
Cairo
Mount Sinai
EGYPT

WESTERN
SAHARA
SAHARA DESERT
Lake
Nasser
Tropic of Cancer

Red Sea

MAURITANIA
MALI
NIGER
CHAD
Khartoum
ERITREA
Asmera

CAPE
VERDE
ISLANDS
Nouakchott

Dakar
SENEGAL
Bamako
River Niger
BURKINA
Niamey
Ouagadougou
N'Djamena
Lake
Chad
SUDAN
River Nile
DJIBOUTI
Djibouti

THE GAMBIA
GUINEA-BISSAU
Bissau
GUINEA
Conakry
Freetown
SIERRA LEONE
Monrovia
LIBERIA
CÔTE
D'IVOIRE
Lake
Volta
GHANA
Accra
Lomé
Porto Novo
TOGO
BENIN
NIGERIA
Abuja
Lagos
CAMEROON
Yaoundé
CENTRAL
AFRICAN REPUBLIC
Bangui
Addis
Ababa
ETHIOPIA
SOMALIA
Mogadishu

Yamoussoukro
Abidjan
EQUATORIAL
GUINEA
PRINCIPE
AND
SÃO TOMÉ
Libreville
GABON
CONGO
River Zaïre
ZAÏRE
RWANDA
Kigali
UGANDA
Kampala
KENYA
Mount
Kenya
Nairobi
Lake
Victoria
Kilimanjaro
Equator

Brazzaville
Cabinda
Kinshasa
Bujumbura
BURUNDI
Lake
Tanganyika
Dodoma
TANZANIA
Dar es Salaam
Indian
Ocean

Ascension

Luanda
Lake
Malawi
COMOROS

St Helena

ANGOLA
ZAMBIA
Lusaka
River Zambezi
MALAWI
Lilongwe
MADAGASCAR
Antananarivo

Harare
MOZAMBIQUE
Atlantic Ocean

NAMIBIA
Windhoek
ZIMBABWE
Okavango Swamp
NAMIB DESERT
BOTSWANA
KALAHARI
DESERT
Gaborone
Pretoria
Johannesburg
Maputo
Mbabane
SWAZILAND
Tropic of Capricorn

River Orange
River Vaal
Maseru
LESOTHO

REPUBLIC OF
SOUTH AFRICA
Cape Town
Cape of
Good Hope

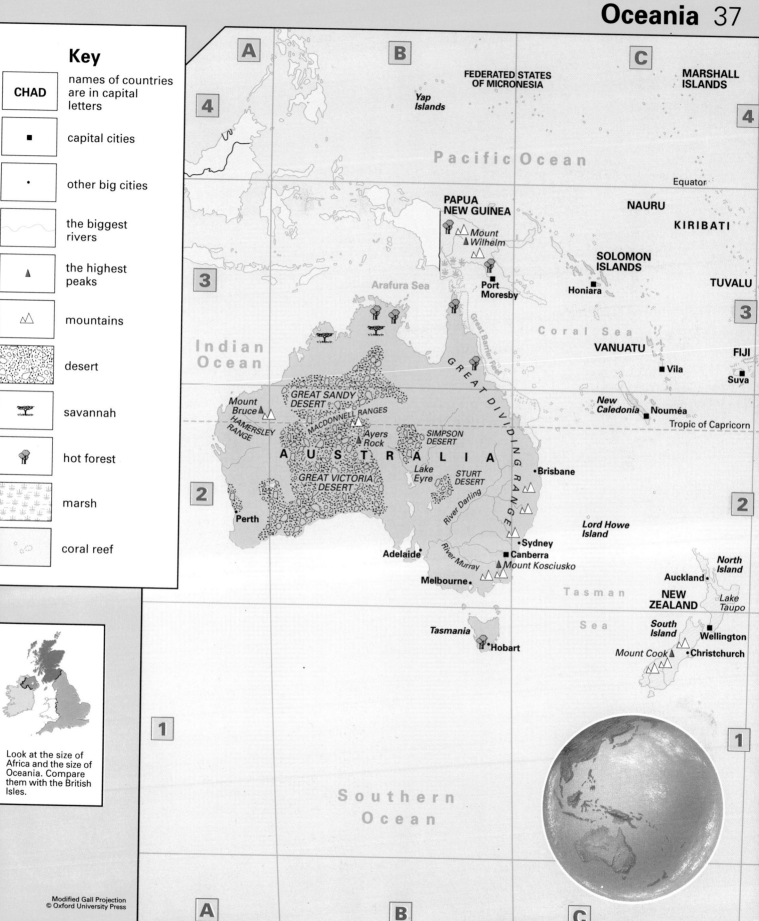

Key

CHAD	names of countries are in capital letters
■	capital cities
•	other big cities
～	the biggest rivers
▲	the highest peaks
⋀⋀	mountains
	desert
	savannah
🌳	hot forest
	marsh
	coral reef

Look at the size of Africa and the size of Oceania. Compare them with the British Isles.

FEDERATED STATES OF MICRONESIA

Yap Islands

MARSHALL ISLANDS

Pacific Ocean

Equator

PAPUA NEW GUINEA

Mount Wilhelm

NAURU

KIRIBATI

SOLOMON ISLANDS

Honiara

TUVALU

Arafura Sea

Port Moresby

Coral Sea

VANUATU

FIJI

Vila

Suva

Indian Ocean

GREAT DIVIDING RANGE

New Caledonia

Nouméa

Tropic of Capricorn

Great Barrier Reef

Mount Bruce
HAMERSLEY RANGE

GREAT SANDY DESERT

MACDONNELL RANGES

Ayers Rock

SIMPSON DESERT

AUSTRALIA

GREAT VICTORIA DESERT

Lake Eyre

STURT DESERT

Brisbane

Lord Howe Island

Perth

River Darling

Sydney

Adelaide

River Murray

Canberra
Mount Kosciusko

North Island

Auckland

Melbourne

Tasman

NEW ZEALAND

Lake Taupo

Tasmania

Sea

South Island

Wellington

Hobart

Mount Cook

Christchurch

Southern Ocean

Modified Gall Projection
© Oxford University Press

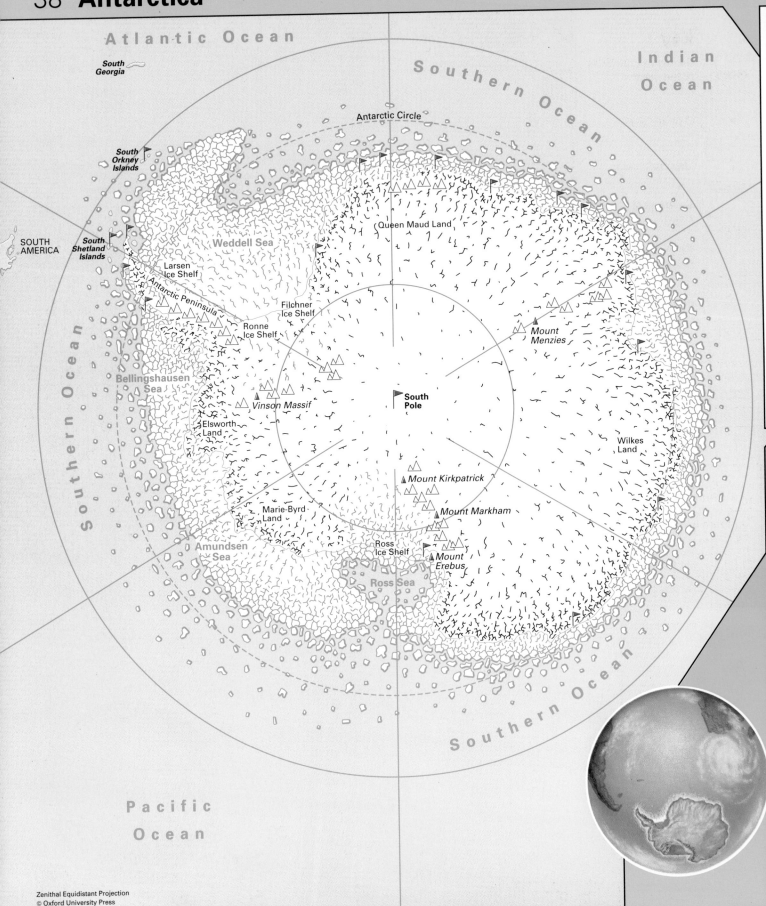

Atlantic Ocean

Indian Ocean

Southern Ocean

South Georgia

Antarctic Circle

South Orkney Islands

SOUTH AMERICA

South Shetland Islands

Weddell Sea

Queen Maud Land

Larsen Ice Shelf

Antarctic Peninsula

Filchner Ice Shelf

Ronne Ice Shelf

Mount Menzies

Bellingshausen Sea

Southern Ocean

South Pole

Vinson Massif

Elsworth Land

Wilkes Land

Mount Kirkpatrick

Marie-Byrd Land

Mount Markham

Amundsen Sea

Ross Ice Shelf

Mount Erebus

Ross Sea

Southern Ocean

Pacific Ocean

Zenithal Equidistant Projection
© Oxford University Press

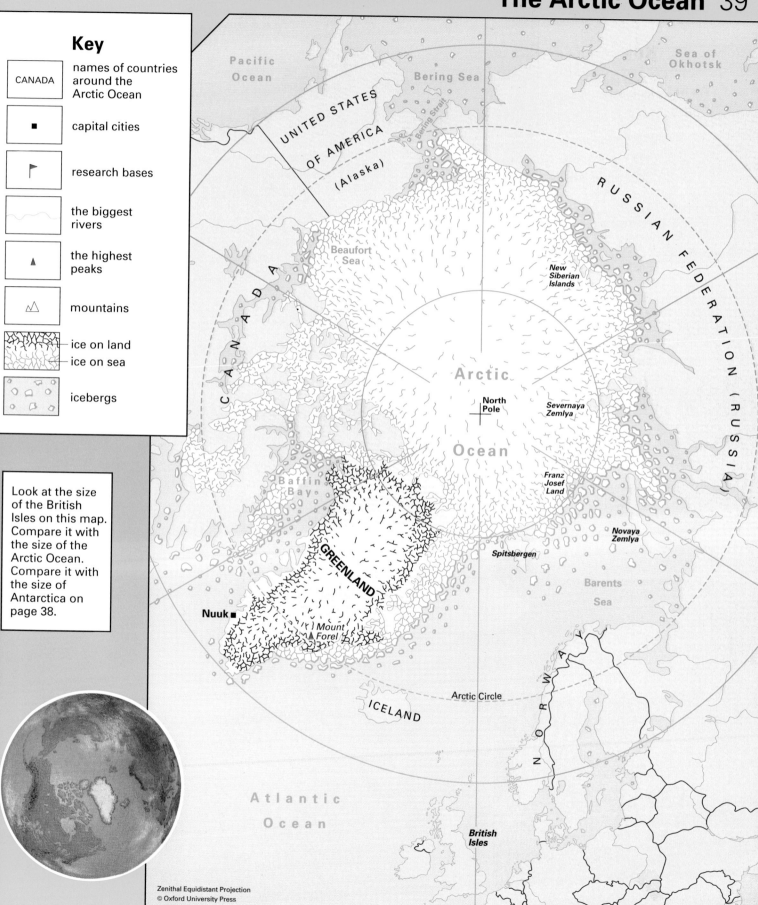

Key

CANADA	names of countries around the Arctic Ocean
■	capital cities
⚑	research bases
	the biggest rivers
▲	the highest peaks
⌃⌃	mountains
	ice on land ice on sea
	icebergs

Look at the size of the British Isles on this map. Compare it with the size of the Arctic Ocean. Compare it with the size of Antarctica on page 38.

Pacific Ocean

Bering Sea

Sea of Okhotsk

UNITED STATES OF AMERICA (Alaska)

Bering Strait

RUSSIAN FEDERATION (RUSSIA)

Beaufort Sea

New Siberian Islands

CANADA

Arctic

North Pole

Severnaya Zemlya

Ocean

Baffin Bay

Franz Josef Land

GREENLAND

Novaya Zemlya

Spitsbergen

Barents Sea

Nuuk ■

▲ Mount Forel

NORWAY

Arctic Circle

ICELAND

Atlantic Ocean

British Isles

Zenithal Equidistant Projection
© Oxford University Press

Key

Asia	continents are named like this
	the biggest rivers
▲	the highest peaks
⋀	mountains
🌲	cold forest
	desert
🌳	savannah
🌳	hot forest
	marsh
	ice on land / ice on sea
	icebergs

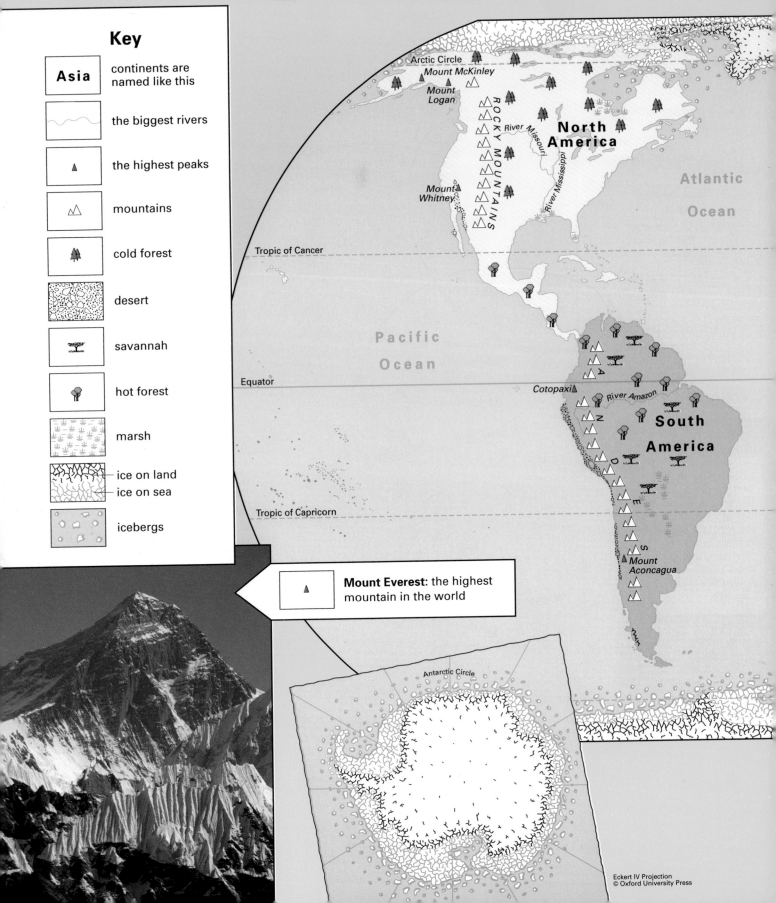

Arctic Circle

Mount McKinley

Mount Logan

ROCKY MOUNTAINS

River Missouri

North America

River Mississippi

Mount Whitney

Atlantic Ocean

Tropic of Cancer

Pacific Ocean

Equator

Cotopaxi ▲

River Amazon

South America

Tropic of Capricorn

A N D E S

Mount Aconcagua

Mount Everest: the highest mountain in the world

Antarctic Circle

Eckert IV Projection
© Oxford University Press

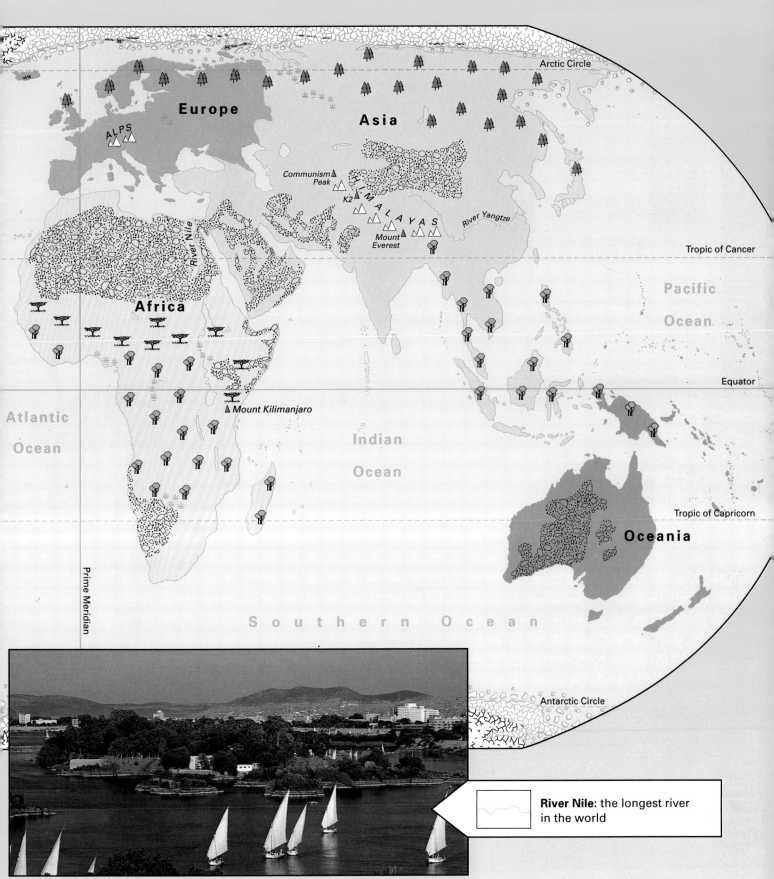

Arctic Circle

Europe

Asia

ALPS

Communism
Peak

K2

HIMALAYAS

River Yangtze

River Nile

Mount
Everest

Tropic of Cancer

Africa

Pacific

Ocean

Equator

Mount Kilimanjaro

Indian

Ocean

Atlantic

Ocean

Tropic of Capricorn

Oceania

Prime Meridian

S o u t h e r n   O c e a n

Antarctic Circle

River Nile: the longest river in the world

Eckert IV Projection
© Oxford University Press

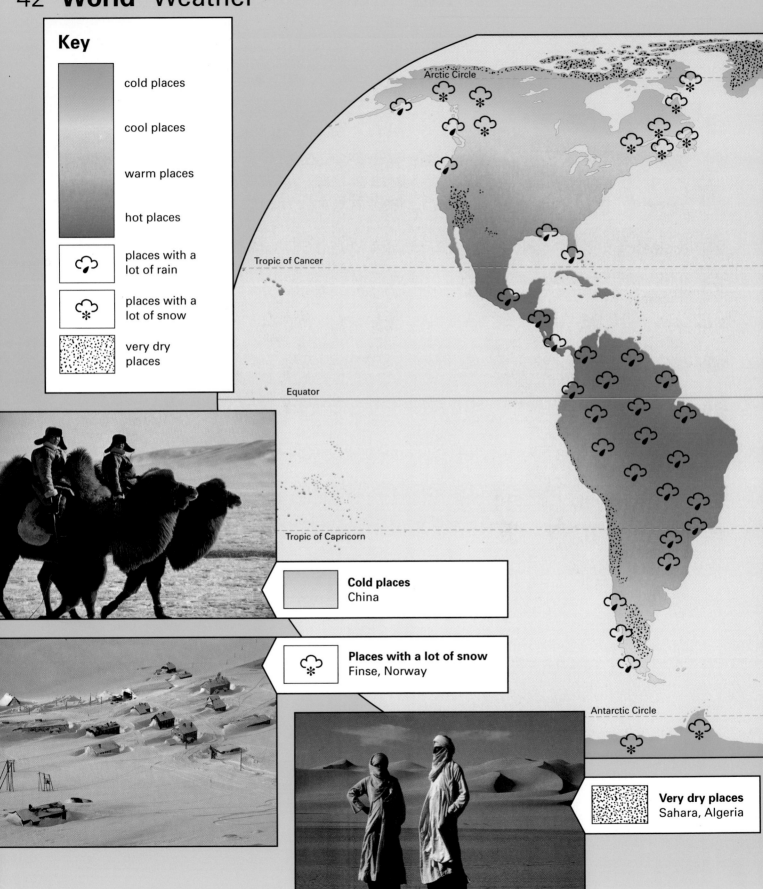

Key

cold places

cool places

warm places

hot places

places with a lot of rain

places with a lot of snow

very dry places

Cold places
China

Places with a lot of snow
Finse, Norway

Very dry places
Sahara, Algeria

Arctic Circle

Tropic of Cancer

Equator

Tropic of Capricorn

Antarctic Circle

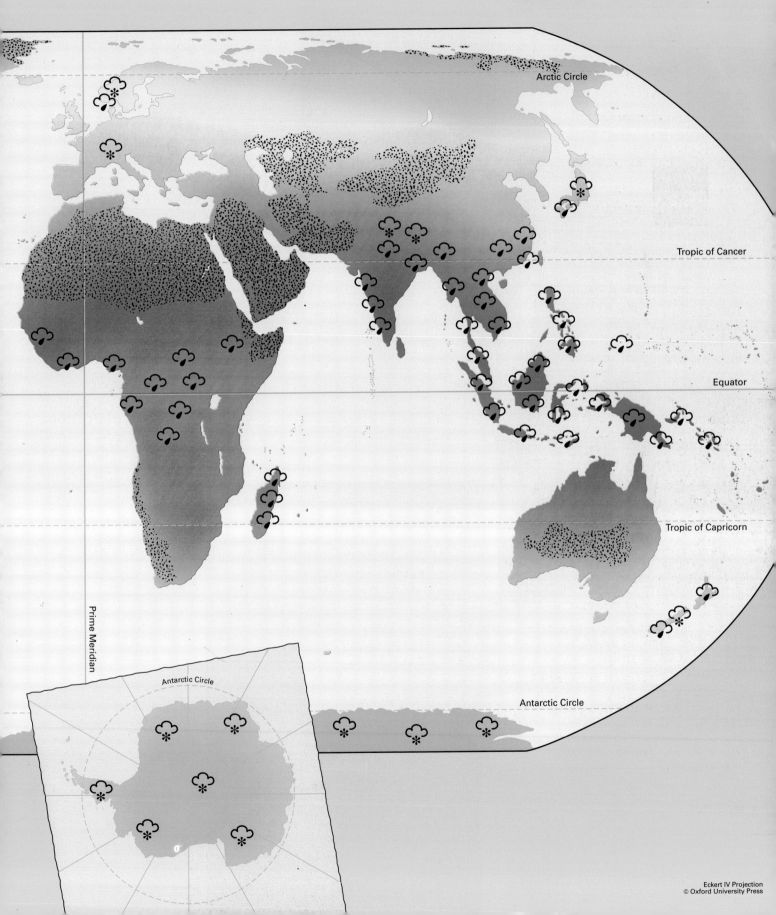

Arctic Circle

Tropic of Cancer

Equator

Tropic of Capricorn

Prime Meridian

Antarctic Circle

Antarctic Circle

Eckert IV Projection
© Oxford University Press

Key

One million (1 000 000) people live near each dot

○ the world's largest cities

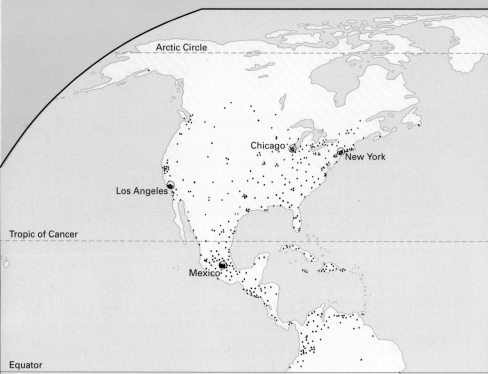

Arctic Circle

Chicago

New York

Los Angeles

Tropic of Cancer

Mexico

Equator

Tropic of Capricorn

São Paulo

Buenos Aires

Antarctic Circle

Places where very many people live. Singapore

Places where very few people live. Shetland Islands, United Kingdom

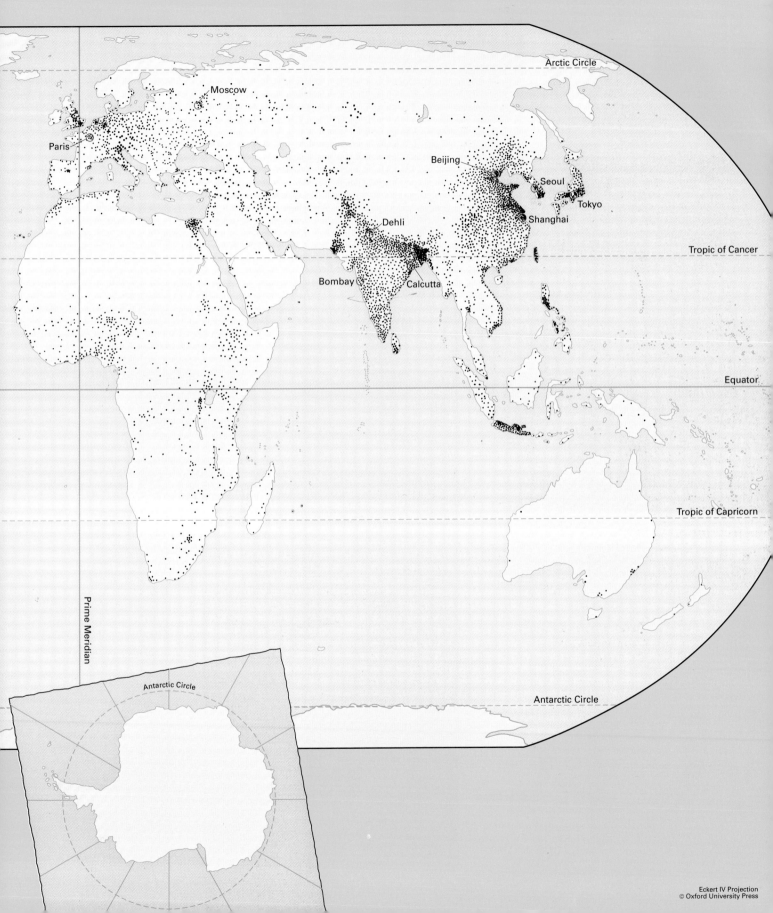

Arctic Circle

Moscow

Paris

Beijing

Seoul

Tokyo

Shanghai

Dehli

Tropic of Cancer

Bombay

Calcutta

Equator

Tropic of Capricorn

Prime Meridian

Antarctic Circle

Antarctic Circle

Eckert IV Projection
© Oxford University Press

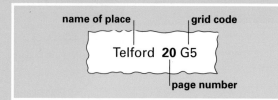

name of place — grid code

Telford **20** G5

page number